Never Forget:
The Story Behind the
Vietnam Veterans
Memorial

Lisa Gough, Editor

Published by:
The Vietnam Veterans Memorial Fund

This book is adapted from material originally written by Kim Murphy and published in *The Wall: 25 Years of Healing and Educating,* a coffee table book created in 2007 to commemorate the 25th anniversary of the Vietnam Veterans Memorial.

For more information, visit the Memorial Fund Web site, *www.vvmf.org,* or the publisher's Web site, *www.mtpublishing.com.* Or call the Memorial Fund at (202) 393-0090.

For more information:

Vietnam Veterans Memorial Fund
1023 15th Street, NW
Second Floor
Washington, DC 20005
(202) 393-0090
Fax: (202) 393-0029
www.vvmf.org
vvmf@vvmf.org

Printed in the United States of America
First Edition
Cover photo by Dan Arant
Back cover photo by Tom Estrin

Table of Contents

Page

Foreword v

The Inspiration 1

The Congressional Mandate 9

The Design Competition 17

The Winning Design 25

The Controversy 33

Construction 43

Additions to the Site 49

The Salute 57

Walkways, Lighting and Long-Term Care 63

The Names 71

Memorial Facts at a Glance .81

Wall Magic. 87

Reconnecting with People You Knew 91
  Charlie Harootunian

Pieces of The Wall. 93
  Nancy Smoyer

The Search for a Name Comes Full Circle. 95
  Arthur Drescher

The Box. 98
  Ron Edgington

A Special Visitor:
The Commander in Chief Pays Tribute. 100

The Future. 103

VVMF Programs. 107

Foreword
By
Jan C. Scruggs

Over the past 25 years, I have observed visitors at the Vietnam Veterans Memorial and listened to their stories. And I have learned many astounding and insightful things.

I once saw a man visiting The Wall wearing Native American clothing. He stood before a panel praying in four different directions, and when he departed, he left behind a pouch. The offering left at The Wall was of significance to his cousin, who was killed in Vietnam, and to his tribe.

It became one of the over 100,000 items that have been left at the Memorial. Each has personal significance to the individual who left it, and each has a story. The phenomenon of so many items being left at The Wall is without precedent and has been studied extensively by talented academicians.

It has been opined that the behavior at The Wall has fundamentally changed the way America mourns. The Wall, it is said, gave license to Americans to mourn in public. The items left at the site of the Oklahoma City bombing and the World Trade Center—even highway markers left to remember those who perished—can be traced to The Wall. There is interaction between the living and the dead at the Memorial, and part of this interaction includes leaving emotionally charged items in tribute.

Many visitors to the Memorial are young people on school trips. Some have heard that the name Rambo is on The Wall. It is, but the Arthur John Rambo whose name is on Panel 16W, Row 126 is not the fictional character portrayed by Sylvester Stallone in the "Rambo" movies. Still, schoolchildren seem drawn to the name of this young man who gave his life decades ago in Vietnam.

Most visitors know little of the history of the Memorial and assume that our government, grateful for the service of its veterans, undertook the time and expense to honor those who risked everything and those who gave their lives in America's longest war. Instead, the veterans themselves built their own memorial as a way to seek societal recognition for their sacrifices.

This book tells that story. The inspiration for the Memorial came from my studies in graduate school. As I saw the need for both individual veterans and the nation as a whole to begin healing from the Vietnam War, I began the effort and enlisted the help of anyone willing to take on the massive amount of work involved. Throughout the effort, we fenced with Congress and some highly entrenched federal agencies, raised money for a project not everyone believed in, dealt with construction issues, solved a national controversy and headed off more daunting challenges than were ever imaginable at the outset.

Astoundingly, the entire effort took just *three years.* The experience was intense. Once The Wall was built, the story even ended up being made into a television movie. My role was portrayed by actor Eric Roberts.

Time marches on, and we came to realize that young people visiting The Wall today were not even alive during the conflict and had no context in which to view the Memorial. And so we embarked on a plan to build an education center near the Memorial. And it has been even more challenging than building The Wall.

Just passing the legislation to authorize the Center took more than three years, despite a grassroots effort involving thousands of teachers, students, business leaders, veterans and even former Presidents Gerald Ford and George H. W. Bush. After years of determined effort, the bill was passed in 2003.

The Center will use the synergy of the nearby Lincoln and Vietnam Veterans Memorials for a profound learning experience unlike anything else in the world. Please visit our Web site, *www.vvmf.org,* to learn more.

This book has some enjoyable reading. I hope you take pleasure in learning more about the history and impact of this amazing work of architecture.

When The Wall was built, the site was selected because of its relationship to the Lincoln Memorial, which stands as a symbol of reconciliation after the Civil War. The war in Vietnam was the most divisive national event since the Civil War, and required similar national healing.

In his book, *Offerings at The Wall,* author Thomas Allen poignantly wrote of The Wall:

"This is a place where memories weave, where hearts heal. This is a place where people can feel what Lincoln called the mystic chords of memory, 'stretching from every battlefield and patriot grave, to every living heart and hearthstone, all over this broad land.'"

I hope that after you read this book, you understand better the significance of The Wall, to the families and friends of those named on it and to all Americans.

The Inspiration

The Inspiration

On Jan. 21, 1970, Jan Scruggs was having his morning cup of coffee, but he was far from his kitchen table at home. He was in Vietnam, serving in the 199th Light Infantry Brigade.

In the nine months since he'd been in-country, Scruggs had already seen a lot of action and had been wounded in a battle near Xuan Loc. He had spent three months recovering in a hospital before being sent back to fight with rocket-propelled grenade fragments permanently embedded in his body.

On that January day, "There was a big explosion," Scruggs recalled. "I ran over to see a truck on fire and a dozen of my friends dying." They had been unloading an ammunition truck when the explosion occurred. Scruggs would never forget the awful scene. He would never forget those friends.

In fact, he would spend a lifetime trying to honor their memory.

The man with the vision

Scruggs was raised in a rural Maryland town between Baltimore and Washington, D.C. His mother was a waitress; his father a milkman. "We're all the result of our upbringing. My background was relatively modest," he said. "But I was always impressed with the example my parents set."

When the 18-year-old Scruggs volunteered to enlist in the Army in 1968, debate surrounding Vietnam was escalating. Its length and the growing number of casualties were fueling tensions. Within months after he recovered from his wounds and returned to his unit, the American public was learning the details of the events at My Lai. By the time he returned home, three months after the explosion, the country was even further divided.

Over the next few years, as the war came to a close and more and more troops returned home, the media began to paint a picture of the stereotypical Vietnam veteran: drug addicted, bitter, discontented and unable to adjust to life back home. Like all stereotypes, this one was unfair.

The truth was, veterans were no more likely to be addicted to drugs than those who did not serve. And if they were bitter, who could blame them? When they returned home from serving their country, there was no national show of gratitude. They were either ignored or shouted at and called vicious names. Veterans frequently found themselves denying their time in Vietnam, never mentioning their service to new friends and acquaintances for fear of the reactions it might elicit.

By June 1977, Scruggs was attending graduate school at American University in Washington, D.C. and had embarked on a research study exploring the social and psychological consequences of Vietnam military duties. He found that returning veterans were finding it hard to trust people. They were feeling alienated from the nation's leaders, and they had low self-esteem. He also found that those veterans whose units experienced high casualty rates were experiencing higher divorce rates and a greater frequency of combat-related dreams. Using his findings, he testified at the Senate hearing on the Veteran's Health Care Amendments Act of 1977, with the hope that he could help veterans gain access to the services and support they needed.

He wanted to find a way to help them heal.

The idea of a memorial

By 1979, the country was beginning to have more positive feelings toward Vietnam veterans. Movies were dealing more realistically with their issues. And Congress was talking about holding a Vietnam Veterans Week to honor those who had returned home.

One film that came out that year, "The Deer Hunter," explored the effects of war on three friends, their families and a tight-knit community. When Scruggs went to see the movie in early 1979, it wasn't the graphic war scenes that haunted him. It was the reminder that the men who died in Vietnam all had faces and names, as well as friends and families who loved them dearly. He could still picture the faces of his 12 buddies, but the passing years were making it harder and harder to remember their names.

That bothered him. It seemed unconscionable that he–or anyone else–should be allowed to forget. For weeks, he obsessed about the idea of building a memorial.

"It just resonated," he explained. "If all of the names could be in one place, these names would have great power—a power to heal. It would have power for individual veterans, but collectively, they would have even greater power to show the enormity of the sacrifices that were made."

His research had proven that post-traumatic stress was real and had shone a light on the challenges faced by a significant number of military veterans. The idea for a memorial seemed like a natural extension of his work and his growing desire to find a way to help veterans.

Making it happen

Scruggs took two weeks off from his job at the Department of Labor to develop the idea further. He had studied the work of psychiatrist Carl Jung, a student of Sigmund Freud, who wrote of shared societal values. As Scruggs analyzed the concept of collective psychological states, he realized that, just as veterans needed psychological healing, so too did the nation.

To make his dream a reality, he planned to get support from people as diverse as former anti-war presidential candidate George McGovern and Gen. William Westmoreland, who commanded U.S. forces in Vietnam. Money was a problem, but Scruggs sold a piece of land he inherited for $2,800—which was enough to hire a lawyer to incorporate the project and hold a press conference.

"The Memorial had several purposes," he explained. "It would help veterans heal. Its mere existence would be societal recognition that their sacrifices were honorable rather than dishonorable. Veterans needed this, and so did the nation. Our country needed something symbolic to help heal our wounds."

Building support

Once Scruggs decided to build the memorial, the next step was to get some people behind him. With Congress still talking about having a Vietnam Veterans Week, he thought that would be a good time to announce his plans. So, he attended a veteran's group meeting.

But instead of receiving help, he was criticized. Veterans told him they didn't want a memorial; they wanted more benefits and government support.

But the meeting gave Scruggs his first ally: former Air Force intelligence offer and attorney Robert Doubek, who thought a memorial was a good idea.

"When I was attending law school, there was no talk at all about Vietnam among the young single professional set of Washington," remembered Doubek. "It seemed unfair and inappropriate that there should be no mention of the war. I really felt what was needed was recognition."

Doubek approached Scruggs after the meeting and suggested that he form a nonprofit organization to formalize his efforts to build a memorial. On April 27, 1979, Doubek incorporated the fledgling group, the Vietnam Veterans Memorial Fund, and Scruggs asked him to join the organization.

One of their first moves was to hold a press conference on Memorial Day to announce their plans to raise $1 million to build a memorial. While media coverage was slim, it prompted a handful of supportive letters and a few small donations.

By July, the Memorial Fund had collected only $144.50, a fact that was reported on the "CBS Evening News" and lampooned on late-night television. This may have seemed a low point for the project, but it caught the notice of someone else who became a valuable ally. John P. "Jack" Wheeler III, a graduate of West Point, Yale Law School and the Harvard Business School, had served in Vietnam. He had also spear-headed the effort to build a Southeast Asia Memorial at West Point. He understood the challenges that building a national memorial would pose.

Wheeler reached out to Scruggs. Although very different from one another, it was clear from their first meeting that the two shared a common vision to honor those who had served in Vietnam and a similar, single-minded "can do" attitude.

The Memorial Fund began recruiting others to help, end-ing up with a group of professional men, all Vietnam or Vietnam-era veterans: George "Sandy" Mayo, Art Mosley, Dick Radez, John Morrison, Paul Haaga, Bill Marr, John Woods and certified public accountant Bob Frank, who agreed to become the Memorial Fund's treasurer. Mayo, Woods and Frank serve on the Memorial Fund's board of directors to this day.

The greatest challenge the Memorial Fund faced, said Doubek, was "to put together a functioning organization with people who didn't know one another, people who were very young and didn't have a lot of experience. We had to constantly find the most effective next step to take and be sure not to get waylaid by tangents."

For Woods, the growing coalition was a prime example of "it's not what you know, it's who you know." These people, though a small group, were able to reach out to their networks and their extensive contacts to recruit the type of expertise and support required for such a mammoth initiative. Their military experience meant they had contacts far and wide, at all levels of all professions, within government and the private sector. It seemed every time they contacted someone, they were greeted with enthusiasm for the idea. Everyone wanted to join the effort. And if they themselves didn't know how to help, they knew someone who did.

Their initial timeline was aggressive, with an ultimate goal of dedicating the Memorial on Veterans Day 1982—just a little more than 36 months away. The list of tasks to achieve such a goal seemed endless. They needed to secure a plot of land, raise funds and public awareness, design the Memorial, coordinate construction and plan the dedication festivities. Most importantly, they needed to navigate the channels of government and do it swiftly.

Never in the history of the United States had a national memorial been conceived, approved, built and dedicated in that short an amount of time. But if the challenges seemed insurmountable, no one expressed any fears. And none of them discussed their own personal feelings or political views regarding the war. All of them realized how critical it was that a memorial be apolitical. They set their sights in support of the clear, simple vision Scruggs outlined: *to honor the warrior and not the war.*

The Congressional Mandate

The Congressional Mandate

When the time came to find support in Congress for the idea, Scruggs decided one of his first calls would be to the senator of his home state of Maryland. But Charles "Mac" Mathias, a Navy veteran of World War II, had been opposed to the war in Vietnam.

Scruggs left a message for the senator, and although the odds were against it, Mathias called to set up a meeting so he could learn more. "I had my ear to the ground," Mathias recalled. "I heard there was a group of serious veterans, not just people getting together to have a beer in the evening, but a group that was serious about getting together to address the problems of the veterans."

Scruggs, Doubek and Wheeler met with Mathias to outline their plans. They stressed that all funds for the Memorial would be raised from private donations. No government funds would be necessary. What they did need, however, was an acceptable location for the Memorial and enough support to push the idea through various governmental committees and agencies.

"Initially the [senator's] staff was split," recalled Monica Healy, a long-time Mathias aide, "on whether Mathias should take the lead and support the efforts to build the Memorial. The senior staffers were against it. It was the senator's gut feeling that we needed to do this."

Mathias had grown increasingly concerned about how veterans had been treated on their return. Because he possessed great knowledge of history, he understood the extensive healing process required after war. A memorial made perfect sense to him. It would be a way to honor the veterans and to help them—and the country—heal.

"This was serious business," Mathias said. "You had to live through that period to really understand it. . . But the veterans had real problems. They needed support, friendship and help. And that message got through to me."

Mathias also knew the country was ready, Healy recalled. Timing is everything, and enough time had passed. Intellectually and emotionally, America could embrace the idea.

In his career, Mathias was cautious, only occasionally being out front on issues. So, when he stepped up not only to support the Memorial, but also to lead the effort, it spoke volumes to those around him.

Choosing the site

One of Mathias' early key suggestions was to bypass the traditional site selection route and have Congress pass legislation to award a specific plot of land to the veterans for use as a memorial site. He identified the ideal spot: a stretch of parkland known as Constitution Gardens, located on the National Mall adjacent to the Lincoln Memorial.

"We got an old Esso gas station map of Washington, D.C., brought it into the waiting room at the Senate Office Building and spread it out on the table," Mathias recalled. "There was a representative from the National Park Service there, and that was when we made the decision."

"He [Mathias] looked at the map, put his finger on the spot and said, 'This is what we want,'" Healy recalled. Mathias wanted the Memorial where the anti-war demonstrations had been.

Enlisting Sen. John Warner

Among other duties, Healy was the member of Mathias' staff who handled memorials and worked as the liaison with the U.S. Department of the Interior. Because of this, Mathias appointed her to manage the details and to work with Scruggs, Doubek and Wheeler on the Vietnam memorial.

The four worked together on a daily basis. "The three of them had different strengths," Healy explained. "Jan was a great spokesperson. Bob was the detail person, who was a good writer. Jack was the visionary, the creative, big-picture guy. They really worked well together and were the driving force. Jack, Jan and Bob were on the Hill every day lobbying. It was such a great cause, and they were bound and determined to make it happen."

As they forged a partnership with Mathias and his staff, the Memorial Fund also set out to establish other key relationships. Scruggs took a bold step in contacting Virginia Sen. John Warner by letter. Scruggs' "can do" spirit appealed to Warner, who had served as Secretary of the Navy during the latter part of Vietnam and was himself a veteran of World War II and the Korean War.

From the outset, having one senator who had been a proponent of the war and one who had opposed the war seemed a critical strategy to the theme of reconciliation. In the instance of Mathias and Warner, both senators were Republicans, but they made a balanced team. Warner was more conservative, able to appeal to staunch Republicans, while Mathias could appeal to the more liberal members of his party, as well as Democrats.

Because Warner was from Virginia and Mathias from Maryland, the two had worked together on many regional issues. They were comfortable with each other, respected one another and knew each other's strengths. "We had been friends for a long time," Mathias said. "He was an excellent partner and fundraiser." Mathias knew the legislative process. Warner, at the time married to Elizabeth Taylor, had strong connections to both Hollywood and the corporate world.

On Nov. 8, 1979, the Memorial Fund held a press conference in which Mathias, Warner and several others announced plans to introduce legislation that would grant two acres of land near the Lincoln Memorial for the Vietnam Veterans Memorial.

Teaming up with the families

Scruggs and Doubek scouted around town, looking for shared office space that might be suitable for the Memorial Fund. They called on Emogene Cupp, then the national president of the American Gold Star Mothers. "Jan and Bob came to our headquarters to see if we had any room to help them get started," Cupp remembered. "We didn't have any space, but I liked their idea and told them I would volunteer to help with all that I could."

The Gold Star Mothers is a group of mothers whose sons or daughters have died serving their country. Their motto is: "Honor the dead by serving the living." Volunteering to assist the Memorial Fund was an ideal opportunity for Cupp to do just that.

Cupp had experienced firsthand the pains caused by the Vietnam War. Her only son Robert had been drafted into the Army. He was killed on his 21st birthday, June 6, 1968, after he stepped on a land mine. Compounding the pain was the fact that society's ill treatment toward veterans extended to their families. "It was very hurtful," Cupp recalled. "They treated the moms the same as they treated the vets. They weren't nice. At that time, they just ignored you and wished you would go away. Or, people would tell me, 'Well why did you let him go?' Of course, what choice do you have?"

A few months after Robert's death, the local Alexandria, Va. chapter of Gold Star Mothers contacted Cupp, who proceeded to become involved in the organization, rising to serve as its head by 1978.

Once Scruggs and Doubek met Cupp, they knew she could be instrumental in helping them communicate the all-important personal, emotional side of the healing story. Cupp began to accompany the two to many of their meetings on Capitol Hill as they drummed up support.

Funding the effort

Just before Christmas 1979, the Memorial Fund embarked on an aggressive fundraising effort led by Warner, who hosted a fundraising breakfast in his Georgetown home that was not easily forgotten by those who attended. Warner made an impassioned plea for funding to his guests, members of the defense industry. As he spoke, all eyes turned toward the staircase.

His then-wife, actress Elizabeth Taylor, walked down the stairs in a regal fashion, wearing a dressing gown, perfect makeup and beautiful shoes that curled up at the toes. "I'm sure I looked like a deer in the headlights, I was so nervous," Scruggs recalled. "I think I even spilled my coffee." But, her presence made a difference. "I heard that those present agreed to double their contributions after Taylor completed her remarks," Scruggs said.

Around the same time, the Memorial Fund also launched its first large-scale direct mail campaign to reach out to the public. To structure these efforts, they formed the National Sponsoring Committee, which included then-first lady Rosalynn Carter, former President Gerald Ford, Bob Hope, future first lady Nancy Reagan, Gen. William C. Westmoreland, USA, future senator James Webb and Adm. James J. Stockdale, USN.

The first fundraising letter was signed by Bob Hope. It echoed the theme that regardless of how anyone felt about the war itself, everyone cared about honoring the men and women who had served and those who had ultimately lost their lives.

By early 1980, contributions started to arrive. Some of the larger early donations came from corporations such as Gruman Aircraft and from such individuals as H. Ross Perot.

Direct mail was proving to be a highly effective fundraising tool. Heartfelt notes written by individuals across the country arrived, accompanied by checks and dollar bills. Letters came from moms, dads, grandparents, sons and daughters. They came from veterans and from the neighbors, teachers, coaches and friends of veterans. The public wanted to have a hand in helping to build the Memorial and in honoring the warrior, not the war.

As work continued, the Memorial Fund realized it needed to increase its fundraising goal. Initially, the target was $1 million. As time went on, everyone realized it would not be enough. The goal was increased to $2.5 million, and staff members stepped up their efforts, often working 12-hour days, six days a week.

Maneuvering through Congress

As the Memorial Fund focused on fundraising, Sens. Mathias and Warner continued to rally support and ferry the legislation. Although there was some opposition to the Memorial from the anti-war movement, Mathias and Warner continually stressed that their objective was to provide the country with a symbol for reconciliation.

"There were so many people helping to get the legislation [passed]," remembered Healy. "The more people you got to co-sponsor, the more people wanted to join."

On April 30, 1980, the Senate approved legislation authorizing the Memorial, followed by approval in the House on May 20, 1980. Both were adopted unanimously. On July 1, a ceremony was held in the White House Rose Garden, where President Jimmy Carter signed legislation providing two acres for the Vietnam Veterans Memorial on the National Mall.

The Design Competition

The Design Competition

With the land approved, the Memorial Fund scrambled to address the issues of what the Memorial would look like and who would design it. A few preliminary concepts were embraced. As Scruggs had always envisioned, the Memorial would feature all of the names of those who had died. Wheeler suggested that it should be a landscaped solution: a peaceful, park-like setting that could exist harmoniously with the Washington Monument and the Lincoln Memorial.

They were also keenly aware that the legislation made the Memorial's design subject to the approval of the Commission of Fine Arts (CFA), the National Capital Planning Commission (NCPC) and the Secretary of the Interior.

It was decided that the Memorial Fund would hold a design competition. Just as the Memorial Fund hoped to help the American people be a part of building the Memorial through their contributions and support, they could also enable all Americans to have an opportunity to participate in its design.

They hired architect Paul Spreiregen to serve as the contest advisor. Spreiregen, a graduate of the MIT School of Architecture and Planning, was a Fulbright Scholar who had served as the director of urban design programs at the American Institute of Architects (AIA) from 1962-66 and as the first director of architecture programs at the National Endowment for the Arts from 1966-70. An author, teacher and lecturer, Spreiregen had conducted extensive research on the subject of design competitions.

At the time, well-managed open design competitions were common in Europe, but not in the United States. Most, like the Lincoln Memorial, were competitions between select designers. Only a few, such as the St. Louis Gateway Arch, part of the Jefferson National Expansion Memorial, had been the result of a well-managed, open competition.

Of his hiring, Spreiregen wrote, "I saw this as a needed opportunity to honor the service and lives of the soldiers we had lost and do so by running a model competition."

For three solid months, Spreiregen, and the Memorial Fund planned the competition. "We had to build credibility among the design community, but also build credibility with the veterans," said Woods. "The design competition also needed to be able to attract design competitors."

There were six phases to the design competition spanning a little more than one year: planning and preparation; launching the competition; the design phase; the design evaluation and selection; the press conference and public presentation; and the public agency approval and project mobilization.

"The first phase encompassed the detail planning and preparations for holding the competition," said Spreiregen. "Holding a competition is like launching a rocket. Everything has to be thought out and in place before the launch button is pressed."

The design criteria

The intention of the Vietnam Veterans Memorial was to honor those who had served and those who had died for their country. The Memorial Fund drafted guidelines for the competition, outlining that each design must: be reflective and contemplative; harmonious with the site, as well as with the Washington Monument and the Lincoln Memorial; contain the names of all who died or remain missing; and make no political statement about war. "The hope is that the creation of the Memorial will begin a healing process," Doubek wrote.

Healing meant many things to many people. Could a memorial accomplish such an enormous and daunting task? Could it heal the chasm within society, promote closure, show gratitude to those who served, comfort those in grief and remind future generations of the toll wrought by war? Moreover, could it accomplish all of that while listing the approximately 58,000 names in an artistic, meaningful way?

Selecting the jury

Selecting a design that would meet the criteria demanded a jury that could grasp the significance of the Memorial's purpose and understand the unique needs of Vietnam veterans, their families and a country divided.

For weeks, heated discussions took place around the topic of who should be part of the design jury. Many felt it should be composed primarily of veterans; others felt it should be made up only of professionals; some thought a mix of the two would be best.

Board member Art Mosley researched the topic. Based on what he learned, he was adamant about having an all-professional jury. Ultimately, the Memorial Fund board followed Mosley's advice.

Spreiregen recommended eight people, seven of whom were to be selected. There were two professionals representing the fields of architecture and landscape architects; three representing the world of sculpture; and one who was a journalist with extensive experience writing about architecture and landscape design. It was expected that only two of the sculptors would be chosen to sit on the panel.

Before being selected, each candidate was required to read *Fields of Fire* and *A Rumor of War*, the current literature on Vietnam. In addition, Spreiregen suggested that all eight have the opportunity to meet with the Memorial Fund board, so that an impartial decision could be reached. The Memorial Fund met the prospective jurors and scrutinized their credentials. "They found that they were very real people who did many of the same things they did," recalled Spreiregen.

"They were real guys. The VVMF group liked them all and approved of them with trust and enthusiasm," even selecting all three sculptors.

The jury included: architects Pietro Belluschi and Harry Weese; landscape architects Hideo Sasaki and Garrett Eckbo; sculptors Costantino Nivola, Richard Hunt and James Rosati; and Grady Clay, journalist and editor of *Landscape Architecture*. Four of the eight jurors were themselves veterans of previous wars.

"Many had worked together, some in Washington. They were also the most collegial people, who would deliberate intensely but never argue or posture," Spreiregen remembered.

Launching the competition

With the jury selected, the next task was to announce and promote the competition. In the fall of 1980, the Memorial Fund announced that it would hold a national design competition open to any U.S. citizen who was 18 years or older.

By year's end, it had received 2,573 registrations from individuals and teams. From the registration forms, it was apparent that architects, artists and designers—of all ages and all levels of experience—were planning to participate. They came from all parts of the country and represented every state. By the March 31, 1981 deadline, a total of 1,421 designs had been submitted.

With such an overwhelming response to the competition, logistics became an issue. End-to-end, the total number of submissions would have stretched 1-1/3 linear miles. The judging criteria stated explicitly that each submission needed to be hung at eye level for review by the jury. But how and where could all of the submissions be displayed?

Vietnam veteran Joseph Zengerle, then an assistant secretary of the Air Force, volunteered the use of an empty hangar at Andrews Air Force Base. The added component of military security made the location even more attractive, since it could ensure that no anti-war or anti-military groups would try to vandalize or destroy the submissions in protest.

In accordance with the strict competition guidelines, anonymity of all designs was carefully observed. Each contestant sealed his or her name in an envelope and taped it to the back of the submission. The designs were received and processed in a large mail-order warehouse east of Washington. They were unwrapped, number coded, photographed for the record and prepared for display nearby.

Judging the entries

The jury evaluation took place over five days, from April 27 through May 1, 1981. They started by touring the site together, although each had already previously visited the location. Then they returned to Hangar #3 at Andrews Air Force Base to view each of the 1,421 designs individually.

"I had calculated that it was possible to see all of them in a minimum of 3 1/2 hours. The eldest juror, Pietro Belluschi, took a full day," said Sprieregen. "By the end of the first afternoon, one of the jurors, Harry Weese, returned to our impromptu conference lounge and told me, 'Paul, there are two designs out there that could do it.'

"On the second day, the jury examined the designs together, walking the many aisles and stopping at each of the 232 designs that had been flagged by one or more of the jurors, pausing to discuss each design that had been noted. The first cut was further reduced to 90 by midday Wednesday. By Thursday morning, it was down to 39. That afternoon, the winning design was selected," said Spreiregen.

"It was the most thoughtful and thorough discussion of design that I have ever heard, and I have heard many," he recalled.

As an example of their thoroughness, one juror made a sketch showing how easily The Wall could be constructed.

Another noticed that someone might accidentally wander across the grass above The Wall, and accidentally fall over the edge to the ground below. The jury proposed that a low "trip wall" be added on the higher ground, several feet away from the edge, to protect visitors. The trip wall was added to the final design.

With the winning design in hand, Spreiregen had less than 24 hours to craft an explanation of the decision—and the design—that would be suitable for presentation to the Memorial Fund. Throughout the judging process, one of the judges, Grady Clay, had taken meticulous notes of the jury's discussions. Together with Spreiregen, he composed a report based on these thoughtful comments.

"They are a treasure of design insight and included many prescient thoughts as to how the Memorial would likely be experienced," Spreiregen wrote of Clay's notes.

Some of the juror comments included:

"Many people will not comprehend this design until they experience it."

"It will be a better memorial if it's not entirely understood at first."

"Confused times need simple forms."

According to the description of the design concept: "The jury chose a design which will stimulate thought rather than contain it."

The Winning Design

The Winning Design

Design entry number 1026, which was unanimously select-
ed by the jury, belonged to Maya Ying Lin, a 21-year-old
Chinese-American architecture student who was attending
Yale University.

For her senior project, she decided to work with a group
of students studying funereal architecture. The previous
year, she had traveled abroad in Denmark and had been
struck by the way areas within European cities had mul-
tiple uses. Norbrow, in Copenhagen, she explained in an
interview for the Academy of Achievement, was "this
enormous park, probably half the size of Central Park, that
was also a cemetery. . . [In Europe] your cemeteries are
habitable. . . they're parks." When she returned to Yale, her
studies expanded to include the nature of the monument,
what it is and what it should be.

As the group of students began working on their assignments, one of them stumbled on a bulletin announcing
the competition for the Vietnam Veterans Memorial. They
decided to use that as the foundation for their projects,
although Lin had no notion of entering the design in the
competition.

One day, they traveled together to the site of the planned
memorial. There, sitting on the grass as people played
Frisbee nearby, the idea came to her. "I knew it when I saw
the site," she said. "I wanted to cut it open and open up the
earth and polish the earth's edges. Then came the embel-
lishment of the names."

Lin wanted to create a park within a park, a quiet, pro-
tected place for people to reflect. In an interview with *The
Washington Post* years later, she said, "It was a beautiful
park. I didn't want to destroy a living park. [As an architect/
designer] you use the landscape. You don't fight it. You

absorb the landscape. . . When I looked at the site I just knew I wanted something horizontal that took you in, that made you feel safe within the park, yet at the same time reminding you of the dead."

Submitting her design

Within weeks of returning to Yale, after her trip to Constitution Gardens, Lin completed her design as part of her senior project. It consisted of two polished, reflective black granite walls, or arms, in a chevron or expansive "V" shape. Each wall grew, sinking low into the ground, with the earth behind it. One arm pointed directly to the Washington Monument to the east, while the other pointed west to the Lincoln Memorial.

"What the Vietnam Veterans Memorial had to be was about honesty, about dealing up front with individual loss," Lin later explained to the Academy of Achievement. "The most important thing I thought was the acknowledgement of loss. We have to face it. If we can't face death, then we'll never overcome it. So, as opposed to pretending it never happened, you have to look it straight in the eye. Then you can turn around and walk back into the light."

In creating the design, "I deliberately did not read anything about the Vietnam War," Lin recalled. "I really felt the politics of the war eclipsed what happened to the veterans. The politics were irrelevant to what this memorial was. . . there were people on that Wall who were for it. There were people on that Wall who were against it. I wanted to offend neither of them. That was a huge goal. So I did not want to know anything about the politics behind the war."

Critical to her design was the order of the names. "I wanted to honor those we lost in the Vietnam War in the order they were taken from us," she recalled in an essay for the commemorative program for the 25th anniversary of The Wall. "Any returning veteran would be able to find their time of service, sharing their memories of those friends and colleagues they had lost with others who were also there at that time—symbolically and psychologically becoming a part of the Memorial's timeline."

Her professor, Andrus "Andy" Burr, reviewed a clay model of her design. He told her, "You have to make the angle mean something." With Burr's feedback, she revised the design to have the names begin and end at the apex of the walls.

"At the intersection of these walls, on the right side, at the wall's top, is carved the date of the first death. It is followed by the names of those who have died in the war, in chronological order," Lin wrote in the narrative that accompanied the design. "These names continue on this wall, appearing to recede into the earth at the wall's end. The names resume on the left wall, as the wall emerges from the earth, continuing back to the origin, where the date of the last death is carved, at the bottom of this wall. Thus the war's beginning and end meet; the war is 'complete,' coming full circle."

As part of the project review process, Lin presented her design to a room full of visiting architects who critiqued her work. Some felt that she should change the black granite walls to white marble, but she stood firm on her approach.

"By polishing those walls," she wrote 25 years later, "it would reflect your image within those names—making you a part of the Memorial."

With no fanfare, Lin mailed her submission to the competition on the last day it could be postmarked. Her rendering, mixed media on paper mounted on board, had an ethereal quality but lacked the usual details inherent in a professional design.

Unveiling the winner

On Friday, May 1, 1981, Spreiregen and Clay presented the jury's decision to the Memorial Fund.

In part, the jury's official statement read: "Of all the proposals submitted, this most clearly meets the spirit and formal requirements of the program. It is contemplative and reflective. It is superbly harmonious with its site and yet frees the visitors from the noise and traffic of the surrounding city. Its open nature will encourage access in all occasions, at all hours, without barriers. Its siting and materials are simple and forthright.

"This memorial with its wall of names, becomes a place of quiet reflection and a tribute to those who served their nation in difficult times. All who come here can find it a place of healing. This will be a quiet memorial, one that achieves an excellent relationship with both the Lincoln Memorial or Washington Monument and relates the visitor to them. It is uniquely horizontal, entering the earth rather than piercing the sky.

"This is very much a memorial of our own times, one that could not have been achieved in another time and place."

Spreiregen and Clay spent 25 minutes presenting the design to the Memorial Fund. "When we concluded, there was a brief moment of silence," Spreiregen recalled. "Jan Scruggs got up and said to all, with heartfelt enthusiasm, 'I like it.' Immediately the whole group jumped to their feet and started hugging each other in joy. They really got it. They really understood what the memorial design was all about, why we recommended it."

"A lot of excitement had built up, a lot of work led up to the design competition. When we heard that the jury had selected one, it was very exciting to get in the car and go over there to see it," Scruggs recalled of that day.

"It was a design that was difficult to understand until the jury explained it to you," he added. "That became the problem, really. That's why others took issue with it, and I can see their point. The average person does not have the skill set to look at something in two-dimensional art and fast-forward to what it will look like as a 400-foot structure. But it was apparent to me that it would be a very handsome stone with qualities that other stones would not have, for example, that you could see your own reflection in the names."

When Scruggs learned that the designer was Maya Ying Lin, a name of obvious Asian descent, he was relieved. "It showed that the design process was fair, that it had worked, that the background of the person was irrelevant" to the selection of a winner, he said.

Woods remembered that day as well, "We were dumb-founded that there was a unanimous decision by the jury. To get artists to agree is unreal.

"They showed us the top three designs," he recalled. "I don't remember the third one, but I remember that the second place winner was a traditional war memorial that glorified war. Then they showed us these pastels that Maya had produced. But it was her description of what she was portraying that had so much meaning. . . this simple, elegant solution.

"Maya's thought was that The Wall was only one element of the Memorial," Woods continued. "The whole Memorial was the entire park-like setting. Each person [who visits] is part of the Memorial. My reflection becomes part of the Memorial. I can think back as I look at the walls. She designed it to be contemplative."

Announcing the winner

With the design selected, attention turned to announcing the winner. It was felt that Lin's renderings were not sufficient for public debut at a press conference. As a few representatives from the Memorial Fund headed to Yale to notify Lin and ask that she return with them to Washington for the press conference, Spreiregen worked with juror Harry Weese's office to create two models of the display. One model depicted the Memorial and its placement within the context of the Mall; the other showed the Memorial design itself.

Once the models were complete, they photographed them and created a presentation slide show, as well as press kit materials. "We realized that the story was to be as much about Lin as it was the design," Spreiregen said. "The press conference would have to be love at first sight or the project was dead in the water."

On May 6, 1981, a press conference was held in a crowded board room at the headquarters of the American Institute of Architects. It was a tremendous success, generating numerous positive national news stories and television reports.

Within days, the annual Armed Forces weekend was held at Andrews Air Force Base. On Saturday, May 9, the doors to Hangar #3 were opened so that the public could view all of the design submissions. A crowd filled the hangar the entire time.

The Controversy

The Controversy

Early on in the effort to get the Memorial built, there were traces of controversy. Some felt that the money to build a memorial could be better spent delivering the many services veterans needed. Others questioned the intent of the Memorial.

Throughout, Scruggs embraced the discourse. Only by no longer ignoring the war and its veterans could the country truly begin to heal. Besides, the controversy helped draw attention to the Memorial, something that was critical to fundraising.

Months before the design competition commenced, the Memorial Fund realized that it once again needed to increase its budget figures, to as much as $7 million in order to fund a memorial fully. The pressure was on for board members, staff and volunteers, particularly for Sandie Fauriol, the woman hired to lead the fundraising effort.

At the same time, grassroots efforts to raise money were beginning to sprout across the country. Organizations such as The American Legion, the Veterans of Foreign Wars (VFW) and the American Gold Star Mothers threw their support behind the effort. Many gave large donations. Children in schools took up collections, and individuals across America continued to give.

When the Memorial Fund announced the selection of Lin's design, the initial public reaction was overwhelmingly positive. "We were finally getting the attention from the media that we had sought from the beginning," Doubek wrote. "Though the unconventional design provoked some negative comment, a consensus favoring its elegant simplicity emerged on the part of the architectural critics, the staffs of the approval bodies and veterans organizations."

But several weeks after the announcement, a handful of people began to protest the design. A few of the most vocal opponents, James Webb and H. Ross Perot, had previously been strong supporters of a memorial. They complained about the walls being black. They did not like the idea that it was below ground level. They did not like its minimalist design. They felt it was a slap in the face to those who had served because it did not contain traditional symbols honoring service, courage and sacrifice. Some opponents simply did not like the fact that Lin was a young student, a woman and a Chinese-American; how in the world could she possibly know how to honor the service of the Vietnam veteran?

Then, in October 1980, veteran and writer Tom Carhart, also a former supporter, testified before the Commission of Fine Arts (CFA) against the design, saying that "One needs no artistic education to see this design for what it is, a black trench that scars the Mall. Black walls, the universal color of shame and sorrow and degradation."

He followed that appearance with an article in the *New York Times*. The media pounced on the controversy and helped his phrase, the "black gash of shame and sorrow," sprout wings.

From the first moment he saw Lin's design during the jury's presentation, Scruggs said, "I was convinced that we had some public relations challenges ahead and some controversy, although I didn't really predict it would spin out of control. The opposition was a small group of influential people who were very good at politics. But they were not alone in their views. They represented many other people who didn't understand the design."

While the controversy made headlines, it also made fundraising easier. The Veterans of Foreign Wars (VFW) began promoting the idea of the Memorial and soliciting donations from their local posts through direct mail. At that time, there were between 9,000 to 10,000 local VFW posts. According to Doubek, by December, VFW presented a check for $180,000. (Over the course of the entire effort, VFW contributed as much as $300,000 through a combination of donations from individual members and the organization.) The American Legion was also busy raising funds and was quickly approaching its $1 million goal.

While Memorial Fund staffers were relieved that donations were pouring in, they struggled with how to react to the escalating controversy. There was no arguing that both sides wanted a memorial. Their goals were the same. At issue was what *type* of memorial would be most fitting. The greatest risk, Doubek felt, was that if they lost the battle to build the Lin design, they would lose the memorial entirely. "The strong consensus and momentum could never be regained, as each new design proposal would be second-guessed for decades," he stated.

"We talked about it [the controversy] constantly," Jan's wife, Becky Scruggs, recalled. "At times, I tried to help Jan keep things in perspective. Other times, I got emotional at what was happening. It was very much a rollercoaster ride. Although, I actually found it to be exciting, the ups and downs of it, occasionally it was overwhelming . . . but the good times outweighed the bad."

Lin also struggled with how to handle the controversy. Her relationships with many of those involved were precarious and strained. As discussions began on the construction of the Memorial, she wanted an ally in the process, someone she could trust to fight for her design. She approached a contact at the Yale School of Architecture and asked for a recommendation of a firm in Washington who could join the project. He suggested the Cooper-Lecky partnership. The Memorial Fund interviewed several firms, eventually selecting Cooper-Lecky and hiring Lin as the project's design consultant.

Bill Lecky recalled the first time he and his partner Kent Cooper saw Lin's design. "We thought it was a very powerful, elegant statement," he said. "There was a page of writing included on her presentation boards that was a beautifully written description of the experience of going to the Memorial. I'm sure that writing ultimately got her the award."

Unfortunately, such eloquent descriptions had done nothing to sway the opposition's opinion. It appeared the opposition might have the power to halt the project in its tracks, despite the fact that the design had been approved by the Commission of Fine Arts (CFA) and the National Capital Planning Commission (NCPC). "We had obtained preliminary approval in just over two months since the design had been procured," said Spreiregen. "Compared to any other recent memorial effort, this was something of a record."

"What I didn't realize at the time," Healy recalled, "was how one small group is all it takes" to shut down an entire initiative. "The opponents were skillful and smart in knowing who to call and how to stop it."

"We thought it would be received by the public with great admiration and understanding," said Mathias. "We didn't know it was going to be quite as controversial as it was. We had a tough time with some of the original donors to the Fund, who wanted to have [the Memorial reflect] their personal ideas of what they thought it should look like."

Reaching a compromise

By early 1982, the Memorial Fund asked Warner to bring together both sides for a closed-door session to hammer out the issues.

A Feb. 22, 1982 article by Hugh Sidey in *TIME* magazine described the session: "A few days ago, 40 supporters and critics of the memorial gathered to try to break the impasse that threatened the memorial because of such features as the black color of the stone and its position below ground level. After listening for a while, Brigadier General George Price, retired, stood in quiet rage and said, 'I am sick and tired of calling black a color of shame.' General Price, who lived with and advised the 1st Vietnamese Infantry Division, is black."

In fact, Gen. Price's speech that day ended the controversy over the black granite and the use of the term "black gash of shame" forever.

To Heal a Nation, the book written by Jan Scruggs and Joel Swerdlow that tells the story of the building of The Wall, gives a vivid sketch of the scene:

"'I have heard your arguments,'" General George Price, one of America's highest ranking black officers said. 'I remind all of you of Martin Luther King, who fought for justice for all Americans. Black is not a color of shame. I am tired of hearing it called such by you. Color meant nothing on the battlefields of Korea and Vietnam. We are all equal in combat. Color should mean nothing now.'"

Sidey's *TIME* magazine piece continued: "At the end of five hours and much shouting, General Mike Davison, retired, who led the Cambodian incursion in 1970, proposed a compromise: add the figure of a soldier in front of the long granite walls that will bear the 57,709 names of those who died or are missing and the tribute to all who served. The battle was suddenly over."

Gen. Price had been working with the Memorial Fund since its earlier days. "These young men finally got to me," he said of that moment when he stood up to put a stop to the color debate. "Black was not a color of shame. We had proven that over and over again. . . and I also resented the fact that anyone would discuss Maya Lin's heritage in terms of her design."

The Memorial Fund's main goal was to ensure that nothing threatened to "disfigure or destroy the imposing image of the design," Price explained.

A new obstacle

The Memorial Fund agreed to the statue compromise, as well as to adding a flag and an inscription on the Memorial, but they did not want to wait until a statue was designed before breaking ground. Waiting meant they would never reach their Nov. 11 dedication deadline.

Both sides worried that CFA and NCPC, who had ultimate approval of the flag and statue, might not support the addition of such elements. Breaking ground while the compromise was negotiated would allow them to proceed.

Yet some wondered whether that meant the Memorial would get built while the statue and flag languished eternally in the approval process. Then, Secretary of the Interior James Watt dealt the Memorial Fund a crushing blow. He threatened not to issue a construction permit unless both CFA and NCPC approved the compromise.

Over several tense weeks, more debate followed, until CFA and NCPC gave their approval for a statue and flag, pending suitable placement of those elements. Watt followed on March 11, 1982 by granting permission for the construction permits.

"No matter how many obstacles there are, if the cause is right, you have to keep going," Healy said of the many lessons learned from that time.

The design's merits overcame the critics, said Mathias. "I'm glad we hung on and prevailed. It was a remarkable exercise in dedication on the part of the veterans," he added. "They were not without differences of opinion, but they were all resolved in favor of the Memorial. . . I've been involved with many organizations, but very few have shown the level of personal commitment that was shown."

With permit in hand, Scruggs met a construction crew at the site. "Make this place look like an airstrike was called in," he instructed. "Rip it apart." His reasoning was that a complete mess would make it tough to stop construction.

An official groundbreaking ceremony was held on March 26, 1982. Sen. Warner's assistant, Andy Wahlquist, had an idea. Get 100 veterans—two from each state—and give them shovels to break ground. Gen. Price, along with Sens. Warner and Mathias and future Sen. Chuck Hagel, gave moving addresses before the command was given, and 100 shovels entered the ground with enthusiastic veterans enjoying the moment.

But, much work was still ahead. They now had only eight months to build The Wall.

Construction

Construction

Not long after Lin's design was chosen, the Memorial Fund began to consider the all-important details of building The Wall.

Memorial Fund board member John Woods, who is an engineer, remembered scrutinizing the design from a structural engineering point of view. He knew it was feasible to build; it seemed rather straightforward. "It was going to be a reinforced concrete retaining wall, set on pilings. That was the easy part," Woods said. The hard part was determining how to locate and create the mirror-like polished stone, how to engrave the names and how to install the granite.

"The initial design was more of an idea," said Bill Lecky of the Cooper-Lecky architectural firm. "The actual details—how long the walls were, how many names were on each panel—came out of the [design-build] process."

Choosing the granite

The challenges that needed to be addressed were numerous. Working with the construction contractor, Gilbane Building Company, Cooper-Lecky had to locate the appropriate type of granite: a flawless, reflective, deep ebony stone. "We went on a worldwide search for black granite," Lecky said. "We uncovered five potential stones. One in Bolivia was believed to be too soft. One in Canada was not black enough. One in South Africa was rejected for political reasons. That left one in Sweden and one in India which were felt to be acceptable."

After bids were received from both, the quarry in India was selected. One of the requirements for the project was that the mine could not use explosives to extract the stone, because Cooper-Lecky did not want to risk having it be cracked and flawed. "I have these images of boulders the size of an

SUV being dragged out of the mine before being shipped to Baltimore and New York, then trucked to Barre, Vermont, where the stones were cut and polished," Lecky said.

Finalizing the size

In addition to locating the stone, Cooper-Lecky needed to design the Memorial to be accessible to people with disabilities, calculating just the right angle of the slope. It was set at a 5 percent slope, the maximum allowed without requiring handrails.

The architects also needed to determine the size of each concrete panel, the size of the lettering and the height of spacing between the lines of names. "If you increase the letter size by one-eighth of an inch, all of a sudden, The Wall gets 25 feet longer," said Lecky. "We performed a graphic analysis to determine how big and how tall the walls needed to be."

Ultimately, one of the greatest challenges was how to get that many names on the wall panels in such a short period of time.

Inscribing the names

"Maya Lin's idea was to have all of the names individually hand-chiseled in the stone," explained Bob Doubek. "One stone carver estimated that it would take every craftsman in the world three years and $10 million to do that." Together, the Memorial Fund and Cooper-Lecky searched for a way for the names to be sandblasted rather than hand carved. They needed to figure out how to make stencils for the names and find a sandblasting technique that would not damage the granite.

In August 1982, the Memorial Fund received a call from Larry Century, a young inventor from Cleveland, Ohio, who had read about Maya Lin's design and had devised a process that could be used to inscribe the names. The Memorial Fund sent him some designs and stone, to see if he could provide a sample. They came back perfectly designed.

Century was selected to serve as a consultant to Binswanger Glass Company in Memphis, Tenn., which was awarded the contract for inscribing the names.

The process began with a photo-positive image of the names, printed on transparent paper—one for each panel. A liquid solution resembling mustard was spread evenly onto a panel and allowed to harden. The photo-positive of the names was mounted on top of the hardened solution, which operated much like photographic print paper. The panel was then rolled into a light booth and blasted with an intense amount of light.

Once the panel was wheeled out of the booth, the photo-positive was removed, and the panel was hosed off with water. The "mustard" solution would melt away wherever the names appeared in the photo-positive, leaving sharp, clean-edged letters which looked as if they had been cut out with an X-Acto knife blade.

The panels were then sandblasted with aluminum oxide and sand. Once the blasting was completed, the panels were delicately wiped with bleach to remove any remnants of the matrix, leaving the polished granite panels with beautifully etched names.

Initially, the process required a few refinements. "When we did the first few panels, they looked great," Lecky recalled. "Then we asked them to move the panels out into the sun. When we saw them in the sun they were disastrous. You could see these rivers of shadows running through the names. It was clear that the blasting had not been done evenly, with some of the letters etched deeply into the stone, while others were very lightly embossed."

To ensure that the sandblasting step was done with even amounts of pressure and force, the team designed a spray booth with a rolling guide, constructed with a series of holes.

The sandblasting nozzle was placed through the upper hole of the guide, then rolled evenly and smoothly across a panel. Workers would walk back and forth, moving the nozzle to each subsequent hole, being careful to maintain the same measured pace.

The process continued through the lowest and last hole, ensuring a consistent blasting depth over the entire panel. Once in place, the process, though crude, worked to perfection.

Additions to the Site

Additions to the Site

In early April 1982, as construction crews tore up turf on the Mall, the Memorial Fund created an independent panel to ensure the successful selection of a statue and eliminate any threat of controversy during its design. The panelists were James Webb and Milt Copulos, who opposed Lin's design, and Art Mosley and Bill Jayne, who supported it. The four would have to arrive at a consensus in order to please both sides.

Jayne had worked as a volunteer for the Memorial Fund early on, focused on public relations. That work led to a job opportunity within the government. In order to avoid any conflicts of interest, he scaled back his time with the Memorial Fund, but maintained his contact with Scruggs and the group. Jayne was also a combat veteran during the Tet Offensive and had been wounded.

"Like most people, I was very impressed by the Memorial's design," Jayne recalled, "[the] way it conveyed all of the names without seeming to bore people. It didn't become a 'yellow pages,' it was more than a directory. I personally was stymied by how to convey all of those names. I was also impressed with the idea of the polished black granite being reflective, [so that] people would see themselves in it. Plus, it meant a lot the way it connected the Vietnam experience with American history, the way it pointed to the Washington Monument and the Lincoln Memorial."

Because of his work on behalf of and his belief in the Memorial, Jayne felt honored to be asked to join the sculpture panel. "I wanted to do everything possible to smooth out the controversy, which was very disheartening and worrisome to everyone."

The Three Servicemen Statue

The panel contacted Frederick Hart, a well-known and respected sculptor whose team had placed third in the open design competition. While conducting research prior to entering the design competition, Hart had spent an enormous amount of time studying Vietnam and interviewing veterans. During that time, he cultivated relationships with Scruggs, Doubek, Wheeler and Webb.

"We weren't sure how we were going to forge ahead," Jayne said. "We talked a lot with Hart and ended up meeting several times at his studio. It was neutral ground and was easily accessible. We talked about what the sculpture should accomplish."

The panel's hope was that Hart's creation would be "representational, true to life, and in effect, put a face on the names," said Jayne.

Hart's early models involved a single soldier, which appeared too lonely. After several meetings and discussions, Hart delivered a model featuring three figures. Immediately, the group knew it was the ideal concept. "My original thought was: 'Our work is done. This is going to do it,'" said Jayne.

From there, they worked with Hart to add the appropriate level of detail which would resonate with veterans. Webb had kept a pair of old jungle boots that Hart used as a reference. Webb also obtained some authentic combat gear for Hart to study. "On the figures, there are different kinds of flak jackets," explained Jayne. "One has on a Marine jacket, with its plates more obvious, while the other wears an Army-styled jacket, and one isn't wearing a jacket." There are other details that are true to service in Vietnam, as well.

On Sept. 20, a model of the sculpture was unveiled to the public. The final piece, known as "The Three Servicemen," is a slightly larger-than-life depiction of three infantrymen cast in bronze. The men—one white, one black and one Hispanic—are all in uniform, carrying weapons.

Hart said this in describing the sculpture: "They are young. The contrast between the innocence of their youth and the weapons of war underscores the poignancy of their sacrifice. There is about them the physical contact and sense of unity that bespeaks the bonds of love and sacrifice that is the nature of men at war. . . Their strength and their vulnerability are both evident."

Lin strongly opposed the addition of both the statue and the flag. Supporters of the statue and the flag wanted to have the flag at the vertex and the statue in the angle, Doubek recalled, in effect making The Wall a pedestal for the flagpole and a backdrop for the sculpture. Rather than viewing them as additions, Lin regarded them as changes that violated the integrity of her work and altered the entire nature of the Memorial. The Memorial Fund was caught in the crossfire between political critics and various factions of the arts community.

After enduring months of controversy and the frenzied construction process, Lin grew weary and resigned from the project.

On Oct. 12, 1982, just weeks before the Memorial's dedication ceremony was to take place, CFA recommended that the flag be grouped with the statue in order to enhance the entrance to the site.

To find just the right location for the statue and the flag, a team from Cooper-Lecky went to the Memorial grounds. "We kept backing away from the apex until we felt we had a location that was suitable," remembered Lecky. It was a location that gave the impression that the figures were emerging from a grove of trees and happening upon The Wall.

Once they determined the location for the statue, the Cooper-Lecky team reworked the walkway system, so that the flag could be placed at an intersection in order to create an entranceway. Today, the 12-foot-by-8-foot flag flies from a 60-foot pole, 24 hours a day, seven days a week, in honor of the men and women who served in Vietnam. The flagstaff, paid for by donations from The American Legion, features an inscription and the seals of the five branches of military service at its base: Air Force, Army, Coast Guard, Marine Corps and Navy.

The completed statue was unveiled on Nov. 8, 1984. "With 20/20 hindsight, the statue now seems like a good addition to the site," Doubek conceded. "A lot of people seem to really find it to be an affirmation, the literal depiction of their youth and courage."

Although the Memorial Fund held a National Salute to Vietnam Veterans in 1982 that included the dedication of The Wall, the Vietnam Veterans Memorial was not officially turned over to the government until the statue and flagpole were in place in 1984. In a Veterans Day ceremony at The Wall that year, President Ronald Reagan and First Lady Nancy Reagan accepted the Vietnam Veterans Memorial from the Memorial Fund on behalf of the American people.

The Vietnam Women's Memorial

While the vast majority of names on The Wall belong to men, there are eight women, all nurses, whose names appear on its panels. Of the 265,000 women who served during Vietnam, nearly 10,000 military women served in-country during the conflict. Barred from combat, these women served in health care, communications, intelligence and administrative positions. Civilian women served as foreign correspondents for news agencies, worked for organizations such as the American Red Cross and the USO, or served in other government agencies, such as USAID or at the embassy.

In late 1983, Diane Carlson Evans, a nurse who served in the Army in Vietnam, conceived of the idea to add a statue to the Vietnam Veterans Memorial to honor the women who served. She incorporated the Vietnam Women's Memorial Project (VWMP) in 1984. In 2002, the group changed its name to the Vietnam Women's Memorial Foundation (VWMF).

According to VWMF, the memorial was established not only to honor those women who served, but also for the families who lost loved ones in the war, so they would know about the women who provided comfort, care and a human touch for those who were suffering and dying.

Ultimately, the Commission of Fine Arts approved a bronze sculpture created by Glenna Goodacre for the Vietnam Women's Memorial. The 2,000 pound, 6-foot 8-inch sculpture portrays three women, one of whom is caring for a wounded male soldier. The composition of the sculpture is interesting and different from all angles. In the surrounding site, eight yellowood trees were planted to symbolize the eight women whose names are on The Wall. The Vietnam Women's Memorial was dedicated on Nov. 11, 1993.

The In Memory Plaque

Years after the war had ended, it became clear that the toll it had taken on those who had served had not ended. Many began to suffer premature deaths related to their service. Some contracted serious illnesses brought on by exposure to Agent Orange. Others endured the consequences of post-traumatic stress disorder.

On Nov. 10, 2004, a plaque was dedicated at the northeast corner of the Three Servicemen Statue plaza, with a ceremony sponsored by the Vietnam Veterans of America. The design team that created the plaque was headed up by James "JC" Cummings, who had worked with Maya Lin in bringing about architectural drawings for her design of The Wall. The plaque is a carved piece of black granite measuring 24 inches by 36 inches. The inscription reads "In memory of the men and women who served in the Vietnam War and later died as a result of their service. We honor and remember their sacrifice."

Since 1999, the Vietnam Veterans Memorial Fund has held an *In Memory* Day ceremony on the third Monday in April to honor all those who died as a result of the war. This yearly ceremony recognizes new honorees and all whose names are on the *In Memory* Honor Roll.

The Salute

The Salute

As soon as groundbreaking for The Wall began in March 1982, so did the planning for its dedication ceremonies. For months, word traveled that a massive National Salute to Vietnam Veterans would take place that Veterans Day. The American Legion, VFW, Disabled American Veterans (DAV), AMVETS and Paralyzed Veterans of America (PVA) made sure their members knew that veterans were going to be honored and welcomed that week on the National Mall. More than 150,000 veterans, families, loved ones and friends made plans to attend.

The series of events began on Wednesday, Nov. 10, 1982 and culminated with the dedication of The Wall on Saturday, Nov. 13.

The Salute opened with a vigil Wednesday morning at the National Cathedral, where all of the nearly 58,000 names on The Wall were read by volunteers around the clock, day and night, through midnight Friday. Every 15 minutes, there was a pause for prayer.

On Saturday, a grand parade took place where veterans marched joyously out of sync, some hand-in-hand or with their arms draped around one another, holding banners, flags and signs. Many pushed friends in wheelchairs. The following week, Kurt Anderson recapped the festivities for *TIME* magazine: "Saturday's three-hour parade down Constitution Avenue, led by [Gen. William] Westmoreland, was the vets' own show. The 15,000 in uniforms and civvies, walked among floats, bands and baton twirlers. The flag-waving crowds even cheered."

Over the four days there were also workshops, parties, events and reunions. "It was like a Woodstock atmosphere in Washington for those who had served in Vietnam," recalled Scruggs. "After three-and-a-half years of nonstop effort and work, with all that you have to do to accomplish what we did, it was beautiful. It was surreal."

"The whole week was extremely emotional," Becky Scruggs remembered. "It was a whirlwind of events, and the press coverage was unbelievable. I remember *The Washington Post* had pages and pages of stories in the 'A' section." Vietnam veterans were, at long last, receiving the recognition they deserved.

Woods remembered, "I was like the kid at FAO Schwartz. I was dumbfounded that we had succeeded at doing this. The controversy overshadowed the mission and what we were doing," until the Salute brought it all together.

After the dedication, Scruggs and Wheeler walked together along the upper side of the Memorial ground, near Constitution Avenue. Although thousands of people were there, "It was so very quiet," Wheeler recalled. "I just kept thinking to myself how quiet it was, and yet there was an immense feeling of community. It was becoming apparent that we had been able to be instruments to something far greater than anything we had ever imagined."

The love and acceptance that the American people gave to the Vietnam Veterans Memorial have continued unabated for over 25 years. Today, The Wall continues to be the most-visited memorial on the National Mall, attracting nearly 4 million people each year.

From the beginning, people have left tributes at its base. Medals, toys, flowers, photographs—anything and everything is left at The Wall as family and friends seek to remember their loved ones who made the ultimate sacrifice in Vietnam.

The National Park Service archives most of the nonperishable items left at The Wall. Every day, park rangers collect and tag the items, noting which Wall panel each item was left beneath. All of these items are stored in a museum-quality facility in Landover, Md. As of December 2006, the Vietnam

Veterans Memorial Collection, as it is called, numbered over 100,000 items.

Maya Lin, has gone on to become a respected designer and artist who owns her own studio in New York City. She is still remembered fondly by veterans for the moving Memorial she designed for them.

"After 25 years, the way in which visitors have embraced and cherished this work has been a great gift to me," she wrote in the program for the 25th anniversary ceremony. "I am always incredibly moved and heartened, especially when a veteran tells me that The Wall has helped them in some way—it could not mean more to me.

"When I meet Vietnam veterans who stop me to say thank you for creating the Memorial, I always want to say: thank *you*, for the service and sacrifices that all of you have made in service to your country," she added.

Walkways, Lighting
and Long-Term Care

Walkways, Lighting and Long-Term Care

"When we were first working on the design, we had no idea it was going to draw the number of people to the site that it does," Lecky explained. "We envisioned people, tourists, walking around with kids, coming across The Wall in the park."

The design intention was for The Wall to rise up seamlessly from the grass, so there were no real provisions for a walkway. However, members of the design team did attempt to address the issue of storm drainage. They designed a sophisticated system which enabled rain to collect and travel down a concrete trough that ran the length of the walls. Narrow concrete slabs with open slats were laid on top of the trough, allowing water to drop down between the slats and drain away.

"The night before the dedication ceremonies, we had two inches of rain," remembered Lecky. "The Memorial looked great the next day; the grass was so lush and green. But when a quarter of a million people showed up, it became a mud bath."

All of the grass died, and soon afterward, the Cooper-Lecky team realized that the sophisticated drainage system had not been installed correctly. All of the turf had to be ripped up and the system reinstalled.

The need for a walkway

During the ceremonies, the team also noticed that visitors to The Wall often stood on top of the drainage slabs as they tried to get close enough to touch the names. But that narrow slab was not sufficient to accommodate foot traffic, nor could the grass withstand it. As a result, when the drainage system was redone, a temporary wooden walkway was erected to meet the needs of visitors better.

Even still, within weeks, it became obvious that traffic at The Wall was going to be much higher than anyone had anticipated. Cooper-Lecky began planning and reworking the paths.

"There were so many people coming. In no time, the National Park Service put up a black chain-link fence so people couldn't walk on the grass," Lecky recalled. "But a few months after the dedication, they called to ask us to widen the path. A few months later, they needed to widen it again."

Lighting the way

It was always hoped that the Memorial would be accessible to visitors 24 hours a day. For the first two years, volunteer veterans kept a nighttime vigil to light the way for visitors.

James "JC" Cummings experienced this volunteer corps first hand. Cummings has served as the architect of record for The Wall since 1997, but in those early days, he was a young architect on the Cooper-Lecky design team. He remembers heading down to the site to handle some business one night. As he got closer to the Memorial, he noticed a Vietnam veteran holding a lantern, escorting a visitor to a name. As the veteran and visitor walked The Wall, the lantern swung gently left to right. Cummings noticed the swinging lantern poignantly reflected in the blackness of The Wall.

"This particular image was the very expression of 'service.' These individuals [were] protecting The Wall, escorting visitors to it, caring for it with such love, and The Wall was reflecting all of that beauty," he explained. For Cummings, that vision captured all that The Wall was intended to be. "I don't know if I'll ever see something that clearly again," he added.

Of course, this was not a long-term solution and, in 1984, a lighting system was installed. It was considered state-of-the-art; however, it required a fair amount of maintenance. Lights were set into the ground near the base of The Wall, and water would leak into various components. Because it was a custom-built system, the replacement parts and bulbs were difficult to order.

By 2004, after 20 years, it was time to update the lighting. An extensive study was conducted to design a system that would be both easier to maintain and would enhance the nighttime experiences at The Wall. The new $1 million lighting system was paid for by the Memorial Fund.

Some of the new lighting was to be set into the paving. But it was discovered that the giant concrete drainage trench had not only twisted, it had also settled and sunk several inches. Replacement drainage and paving systems were necessary. To protect the walls from errant equipment and flying debris, they had to be covered completely during the repairs. Work was done on one side and then the other, so that the entire Memorial did not have to be closed to the public.

During the construction process, as crews hoisted the old pavers, they discovered hundreds of small objects that had been left at The Wall and had fallen through the paving joints. "It was a very moving situation," Cummings recalled. "Something as ordinary as picking up a sidewalk led to finding all of those items." There were notes, religious medals, rings and trinkets. Each day, workers took great care to retrieve the items so they could be catalogued and added to the greater collection.

Caring for The Wall

Today, The Wall has a host of individuals and organizations that care about and for it. The National Park Service is its legal steward, while the Memorial Fund makes significant contributions to assist in its care. "The volunteers at The Wall are the 'first responders,'" Cummings explained. They are intimately familiar with the Memorial and are usually the first to notice when there may be a problem. When they do, they inform NPS or the Memorial Fund, so that a convention of caregivers can meet to determine the best solution.

The Memorial Fund provides insurance for The Wall. In 2005, it paid more than $1 million to install the new lighting system. Annually, the Memorial Fund also pays to have names inscribed on The Wall. In these ways, the Memorial Fund has shared maintenance responsibilities with the National Park Service in a model public/private partnership.

A detailed care manual developed by Cooper-Lecky guides most of the general maintenance. Since the majority of the Memorial is a park setting, much of the maintenance involves lawn care. One year, dandelions threatened to take over the entire grounds. For the Three Servicemen, NPS waxes the statue each Memorial Day and Veterans Day to protect its bronze finish.

The National Park Service organizes and schedules weekly washings of The Wall by groups of volunteers, from April to November when the temperatures are above freezing. The groups consist of student, veteran, civic and community organizations from a variety of locations. Groups contact NPS during the winter in order to secure a date and be placed on the 31-week schedule. On Wall washing day, which is typically a Saturday or Sunday, volunteers meet at The Wall between 6:00 and 6:30 in the morning. A ranger provides them with brooms, hoses, trash bags, nozzles and a brief instructional safety talk. Usually, groups are made up of 10 to 15 people, although on occasion they may be as large as 40.

A few years after the Korean Memorial was completed, it too needed some love and care. On their own, some groups of volunteers have gone to the Korean Memorial to clean it, once they were done at The Wall. To Cummings, the tender care that spilled over to the Korean Memorial demonstrates the powerful, positive impact The Wall has had on its surrounding neighborhood and the community.

The Names

The Planes

The Names

When The Wall was dedicated in 1982, there were 57,939 names inscribed. At the time, approximately 1,300 names were designated as servicemen who were either missing or prisoners of war.

The essence of The Wall is the names and the reaction of the visitor to seeing his or her reflection in this sea of remembrance. Millions come to experience this Memorial each year. Some are drawn to The Wall like pilgrims to Mecca. Others think it is just another tourist stop until they feel the haunting power of this unique work of remembrance designed by Maya Lin, a 21-year-old American.

The order of names

After Lin's design was selected, one of the early debates was whether the names should appear on The Wall in alphabetical or chronological order. Lin's intention from the beginning was to have the names appear chronologically, beginning and ending at the apex. She wanted the names to tell the journey, or the timeline, of the war.

This approach would allow veterans, friends and family members to find a loved one by his or her date of casualty. It would also enable veterans to find groups of friends who died during the same incident. Fallen comrades could be together on The Wall, as they'd been in death.

And there would be nothing to denote service or rank. No single person's service or sacrifice would be any greater than anyone else's. All would be represented equally, with generals listed alongside infantrymen.

Lin's vision prevailed. The names are listed in chronological order, according to the date of casualty. This is "the genius of Maya's design," said Scruggs.

"The chronological order allows veterans who were in a battle to see their friends forever united on The Wall," he explained. "As she wisely predicted, this would help bring the veterans back in time—and a cathartic healing would occur for many by facing this loss again."

Scruggs also pointed out that some common names appear on the Memorial more than once. Chronological order by date of casualty allows friends and family members to pick out their loved one from all of the others with the same name.

The casualty date is the date the person was killed or wounded in combat or injured during an accident; for the missing, the date is when the person was reported missing. The first two names listed on Panel 1, East Wall, at the apex are from July 8, 1959. On that panel, above the names is this inscription:

> *In honor of the men and women of the armed forces of the United States who served in the Vietnam War. The names of those who gave their lives and of those who remain missing are inscribed in the order they were taken from us.*

The last 18 names listed on the bottom of Panel 1, West Wall, also at the apex, are from May 15, 1975. These names are followed by the inscription:

> *Our nation honors the courage, sacrifice and devotion to duty and country of its Vietnam veterans. This memorial was built with private contributions from the American people. November 11, 1982.*

The symbols beside each name

Beside each name is a symbol that denotes a service member's status: either missing or confirmed dead. On the

West Wall, the symbol precedes the name; on the East Wall, the symbol follows the name.

A diamond symbol signifies that the service member's death was confirmed. Those designated by a cross symbol were considered to be missing in action when the war ended. In the event a service member's remains are returned or accounted for, then a diamond symbol is engraved over the cross. Several hundred such designation changes have been made since The Wall was built in 1982. If a service member were to return alive, a circle—the symbol of life—would be inscribed around the cross. However, there have been no such cases.

Selecting names for The Wall

Bob Doubek of the Memorial Fund was tasked with identifying all of the names to be included on The Wall. During and after the Vietnam War, the Department of Defense (DOD) compiled a list of combat zone casualties according to criteria in a 1965 Presidential Executive Order. It specified the geographic areas of Vietnam, Laos, Cambodia and surrounding coastal areas as combat zones. If a person died or went missing in those areas, DOD considered that individual to be a combat zone casualty and eligible for inclusion on The Wall.

Unfortunately, the Department of Defense and the individual service branches maintained separate casualty lists with differing criteria. This was long before the advent of integrated computer databases. The result: no comprehensive master list of Vietnam War casualties existed. Getting the individual branches to cross-reference their information with the DOD list would be impossible. That job would instead fall to Doubek.

Compounding these difficulties was the issue that many casualties, particularly from the Air Force, were not always straightforward in terms of locale. "In order to have your name on The Wall, you had to have died within the 'war zone,'" explained Doubek. "But you had stories of guys in the Air Force who would die in their aircraft over Thailand after having been shot over Vietnam." Technically, they were ineligible for inclusion on The Wall.

For those and a handful of other unique circumstances, Doubek made his own list of men who had died due to their combat experiences—names that may have been listed by an individual service branch, but not by DOD. With this list in hand, he went to the various locations where individual service records were kept, pulling and reviewing each file.

"I looked at the record to determine whether mortal wounds were sustained," Doubek said of the service members whose names were listed by the individual service branches, but not by DOD. He added that he tried to make the best call he could when adding names to the list. Unfortunately, a small number of names of men who were still alive were mistakenly added to The Wall. To put a circle around the symbol beside their names would not provide the correct historical context related to their situation. Their names, however, have been removed from the printed *Directory of Names*.

Ensuring accuracy

Another challenge was ensuring the accuracy of the names. Doubek contacted the National Personnel Records Center, Archives and Records Service, in St. Louis, Mo. On the other end of that phone call was an Air Force officer who had served in Vietnam. He would become instrumental in helping Doubek identify names and check spellings.

Once a master list was compiled, the names were checked manually for errors. "We worked very hard with volunteers from the Gold Star Mothers," recalled Doubek. For weeks and weeks, a team worked through the list, verifying spellings and ensuring that the computer printout that was to be used for the stenciling was correct.

During one review, Doubek found a glitch with the computer software: it did not recognize the spaces that appeared within a last name, such as "van der Meide." It could not properly denote a generational suffix, nor could it discern between a compounded first name, such as Billy Bob, vs. a traditional first and middle name. As a result, the software improperly truncated or abbreviated names. With the glitch discovered, Doubek and his team located and hand-corrected each error.

On the stencil printouts, each line contained five names per row. In some instances, names needed to be shuffled in order to fit on a line. Or, if a name was particularly long, it would be swapped with a shorter name. "I went through the whole list of names eight times, because I was concerned about the correct formatting," remembered Doubek.

Adding names

As of 2007, a total of 317 names had been added since The Wall's dedication. There are now 58,256 names. The first group, added in 1983, included 68 Marines who were killed when their R&R (rest and relaxation) flight crashed in Hong Kong. A few years after the dedication, the issue of geographic criteria was expanded by DOD to include people who had been killed outside of the war zone while on or in support of direct combat missions. This change prompted the addition of 110 names in 1986.

The Vietnam Veterans Memorial Fund receives numerous requests each year from individuals who wish to have particular names added to the Memorial. While the Memorial Fund finances the name additions to The Wall, it is the Department of Defense that makes these difficult and often technical decisions. The Memorial Fund does not have the authority to overrule those who adjudicate these matters.

Once additions are approved by DOD, the Memorial Fund receives the list of approved names, coordinates the inscribing and absorbs the costs.

Names that become eligible for inclusion are added once each year, in May, a few weeks before Memorial Day. Family members are invited to witness the inscription and also to attend the annual Memorial Day ceremony when the new names are read at The Wall.

For families who have worked to have their loved one's name added, the journey can be long and exhausting. Some have tried for years before receiving approval from DOD. Colleen Pontes, whose father Kevin Joyce was added in 2003, remembered the rush of emotions she felt as she and her brother watched their dad's name being inscribed in the granite. "Proving a direct correlation to the injuries is a challenge," Pontes explained. "I respect the process, but it can be hard to prove something that's in your heart."

"That's what makes it so special when you see the name going up," she added. "And they are so respectful when they do the engraving. They seem honored to be putting the names on The Wall."

Jim Lee, formerly of Great Panes Glassworks and now with Engrave Write in Denver, comes every year to add the names to The Wall. Lee sets the artwork, finds places in the margins where each name can fit, tries hard to put each name among comrades and is careful to create a mockup which closely resembles the style and depth of the other names. "They do a really good job making the physical appearance of the names match the original panel," Cummings noted.

Locating a Name

Although the names are not listed alphabetically, it is not difficult for visitors to find a name on the Memorial. The National Park Service offers these steps for locating a name:

1. Look up the name in the Vietnam Veterans Memorial *Directory of Names*. These directories are located at both ends of The Wall and contain an alphabetical listing of all the names on the Memorial.

2. Note the panel and line number for the name listed. The panel number is a number/letter combination, such as 10W or 35E. "W" denotes the west arm of The Wall, and "E" denotes the east arm.

3. Locate the corresponding panel at the Memorial. The west arm of The Wall is on the left when standing at the center facing The Wall. The east arm is the right half. The panels are numbered beginning from the center out toward the ends of The Wall. The panel numbers are inscribed at the bottom of each panel.

4. Locate the line on which the name is inscribed. Count down from the top of the panel. Inscribed dots in the margins of every other panel mark every 10 lines to aid in counting.

National Park Service rangers and volunteers are available to assist in locating names at the Memorial. Names can also be located on The Virtual Wall on the Memorial Fund's Web site, *www.vvmf.org*.

Memorial Facts
at a Glance

Memorial Facts at a Glance

Length

Each of the walls of the Vietnam Veterans Memorial is 246 feet, 8 inches long. They meet at an angle of 125 degrees, 12 minutes, pointing exactly to the northeast corners of the Washington Monument and Lincoln Memorial. The walls are supported along their entire length by 140 concrete pilings driven approximately 35 feet to bedrock.

Height

At their vertex, the walls are 10 feet, 1.5 inches high.

Composition

The stone for the walls, safety curbs and walkways is black granite quarried near Bangalore, India. All cutting and fabrication was done in Barre, Vermont.

Symbols

Each name is preceded (on the West Wall) or followed (on the East Wall) by a symbol designating status. The diamond symbol denotes that the service member's death was confirmed. The cross symbol denotes missing in action. In the event an individual's remains are returned, the diamond symbol is superimposed over the cross.

The names

The original 57,939 names were grit-blasted in Memphis, Tenn., using industrial equipment and stencils produced through a photographic process.

Since 1982, 317 names have been added to The Wall by Denver-based craftsmen using the same photo-generated stencils. The letters are 0.53 inches high and are inscribed to a depth of approximately 0.015 inches.

The names were provided by the Department of Defense, which compiled a list of combat zone casualties according to Presidential Executive Order #11216, handed down by President Lyndon B. Johnson on April 24, 1965. It specified Vietnam and adjacent coastal waters as a combat zone. This zone was expanded to include Laos, Cambodia and Air Force bases in Thailand.

Women
The names of eight women, all nurses, are inscribed on The Wall. Seven are from the U.S. Army; one is from the Air Force.

Medal of Honor recipients
The names of 151 Medal of Honor recipients are on The Wall.

Chaplains
There are 16 clergy members listed on The Wall: seven Catholic, seven Protestant and two Jewish.

People from other countries
There are 120 individuals on The Wall who listed foreign countries as their home of record. The countries include: Australia, Bahamas, Bolivia, Brazil, Canada, Colombia, Costa Rica, England, France, Germany, Ireland, Italy, Jamaica, Japan, Mexico, New Zealand, Pacific Island, Panama, Peru, Philippines, Puerto Rico and Switzerland.

Panel numbering
Each wall has 70 separate panels, plus a panel at each end without names, for a total of 140 panels of names. The list starts and ends at the middle of the Memorial. Beginning with the year 1959 inscribed at the top of the panel on Panel 1 East (1E), the listing goes out to the right, to the end of

the east wall, Panel 70 East (70E). It resumes at the end of the west wall, Panel 70 West (70W), and continues to the right, to Panel 1 West (1W), with 1975 inscribed at the very bottom.

Funding

The Vietnam Veterans Memorial was paid for by donations from more than 275,000 individuals, veterans and civic organizations, corporations, foundations, and unions. No federal funds were used.

Wall Magic

Wall Magic

The Wall has many stories surrounding it—stories of friends who reconnect, of families who meet men who served with their loved ones, of friendships and marriages forged at The Wall. These occurrences come about through events that seem like more than coincidence. These times forge the stories that have come to be called "Wall Magic."

Those who spend a lot of time at The Wall, especially the volunteers who go there every day to assist visitors in finding names and help them through their grief, have seen many instances of Wall Magic. These stories, and there are many, involve improbable coincidences that happened at or because of The Wall.

An early Wall Magic story comes from Bob Doubek, who worked so hard with the Memorial Fund to make the dream of a Memorial a reality. In the final days before the Salute to Vietnam Veterans in 1982, construction and landscaping crews were trying to keep the crowds off of the newly laid sod using fences around the Mall. Doubek was down at the site, wrapping up for the night. A young man approached and asked if he could go down to The Wall. Doubek asked him to return another time. The young man said he was from California and would be leaving soon, so he wouldn't be able to return.

Doubek agreed to walk the man down to The Wall. "As we were walking, I was telling him how the [panels] are like pages in a book. He was getting emotional. I had the directory with me. So we looked up the location of this name, then he thanked me and left."

The morning after the dedication, Doubek and his wife were watching Charles Kuralt on "CBS Sunday Morning." Kuralt traditionally ended the show with a snippet of film, and that day, they were showing footage of the Memorial.

Gradually the camera moved in closer, Doubek recalled, "until you were seeing one wall. . . then 10 panels. . . then one panel. . . then a few rows of names. . . then the camera stopped to focus on a single name. . . and it was the same name that the guy had asked me to see."

He sat stunned for a moment, then thought to himself, "Maybe that guy was an angel telling me I've done OK."

That day, Bob Doubek experienced a little bit of Wall Magic. Following are stories from some long-time volunteers at the Vietnam Veterans Memorial, who have their own stories of coincidental meetings that produced some magic.

Reconnecting with People You Knew
By
Charlie Harootunian

On three occasions, I have been at The Wall when visitors have requested name rubbings of people I knew. One was a Marine who asked for the name of a college classmate of mine who took his ROTC commission in the Marine Corps. The classmate and I were in Vietnam at the same time, but he was killed after five days in-country. I always wondered what had happened to him, and this visitor had wondered about him prior to his entering the Corps. We both provided missing pieces to each other.

When you consider the number of people whose names are on The Wall and the number of visitors to The Wall, the odds are extraordinary that we would meet.

On two other occasions, people asked for the same name of one of the men who served in my platoon who was our first casualty. The first visitor was a neighbor and the second was someone who works with one of his brothers. Both provided a wealth of information about the family and their location. What are the odds of that happening once, never mind twice?

On the 20th anniversary of The Wall, all the names were read in chronological order, taking place over three days. Many volunteers, family members, veterans and citizens took part in the name reading. On the last day, I was working near the stage when I noticed a regular attendee at the Veterans Day ceremonies standing nearby.

I spoke with him for a while and asked him if he had read any names yet. He said that he had not, and it was just something he could not do. He said he was standing around because there were eight men he had served with whose names are on The Wall and he wanted to be there when their names were being read. Just then, someone came up to me and handed me their list of 30 names and apologized, saying they were to read in about a half hour but could not stay. I said it would not be a problem. There were enough volunteers available so that the names would be covered.

Then I handed the sheet to my friend and said that he was going to read the names. He was hesitant, but accepted the list. After about two minutes, his face had a look of shock. I asked what the matter was. He said that the sheet I had given him had five of the eight names on it.

Wall Magic. What are the odds?

Charlie Harootunian is a Vietnam veteran who has volunteered at The Wall since 1986. He lives in Massachusetts.

Pieces of The Wall
By
Nancy Smoyer

- A man stands by a panel where he has placed a large picture frame containing pieces of a boy's life: a picture of the young man in uniform, a newspaper article about him as a football star and one about his death, the letter from his commanding officer to the family. A couple comes up to look at it, and the man says to his wife, "I knew that man. I served with him." The other man hears him and says, "That's my brother."

- A vet is at the information booth trying to locate his buddy's name on the directory computer. He knows the name should be there because he put him onto a chopper, badly wounded, but the name can't be found. While they are searching, another man comes up looking for his buddy's name, which he, too, can't find. He had seen his platoon take devastating mortar fire at the LZ as he was being medevaced out. And then the two men realize that they are looking for each other.

- A woman stands in front of her brother's panel. A man nearby asks a volunteer for six rubbing papers. The woman knows that when her brother was killed, 18 others in his platoon also died, so she asks the man if he was a Marine and if he's looking at the same day. He says yes, he was in the same company, but he doesn't know her brother or the man who died trying to save him. But he has buddies who are on The Wall with them and he was in the area at the time, so he is able to tell her what happened that day.

- Two men see another man doing a rubbing of the same person they are there to visit. When they talk, they find that the man doing the rubbing was his best friend in high school, and the other two were his buddies in Vietnam. The vets say that they would like to get a message to his family, that there are people who still care. They tell the childhood friend that they have both named their first child after their buddy: both girls, both named Chris. The vets ask if the friend would like to know more about how Chris died, and they go off together talking.

- A group of Soviet veterans who fought in Afghanistan come to visit their American comrades with whom they have so much in common in the wars they fought, both in foreign countries and at home. They place a folded flag from their country at the base of The Wall, and standing quietly around it, one by one place a red carnation across the flag. Someone speaks briefly in Russian, and then they slowly disperse. At another time, Soviet Afghan veterans leave a cigarette, a shot glass and a piece of bread: the traditional salute to fallen comrades.

Nancy Smoyer is a volunteer at The Wall. She lives in Fairbanks, Alaska.

The Search for a Name Comes Full Circle

By
Arthur Drescher

On St. Patrick's Day 1973, I met a young woman at a church retreat, and it was special from the moment we met. Her name was Barbara and she lived in Washington, D.C. At the time we met, she was wearing an MIA bracelet for Brian Kent McGar. I didn't know it at the time, but that the bracelet would play an important part in my life more than 20 years later.

It was a whirlwind courtship. We got engaged on June 10 and were married on August 4.

By 1978, we were the proud parents of two sons. Although we lived in Philadelphia, we visited friends and spent time in Washington whenever we could. After the Vietnam Memorial was built in 1982, we would make sure to visit. We tried to find the name from Barbara's bracelet on The Wall, but we could not remember how it was spelled, and we never located it.

Barbara died of breast cancer in September 1986. She never got to see Brian McGar's name on The Wall. But, my sons and I continued to visit Washington, and on one of our visits to The Wall, we found the name. Somehow, it almost felt that Barbara was there, too.

In 1995, on a visit to The Wall, I heard a volunteer couple tell a visitor that they came for a week once or twice a year to work there. That got me to thinking that I could be a volunteer, too.

I worked at The Wall for the first time in December 1996, helping visitors like others had helped my sons and me. It was all I had hoped the experience would be, and more. I found myself driving to Washington as often as I could to work. I sometimes joke that my new wife, Bonnie, would be a "Wall Widow" on weekends if we lived closer to D.C.

In the summer of 2002, I met a social studies teacher from California named Marilyn Wood while I was volunteering at The Wall, and I told her about the Memorial Fund's Teach Vietnam Teachers Network national conference. The first one was held in 2002, over the very week she was visiting. We exchanged e-mail addresses and communicated several times over the next year. The following spring, I found out she would be coming to the 2003 Teachers Conference.

One of the only assignments each teacher had been given before the conference was to find the name of someone on The Wall who had a connection to them and then honor that person the last night of the conference. On the first afternoon of the 2003 conference, a volunteer friend told me he had met Marilyn at The Wall that day. She was working on the computer just then, so I went over to greet her. As I approached, I saw on the screen the name of Brian Kent McGar. I was astonished and asked her why she was looking up information about him. I had never told her about my wife's MIA bracelet. Marilyn told me that she had gone to high school with him, and she was presently teaching in that high school in Ceres, Calif.

I couldn't believe what she had just told me. I had invited a complete stranger to come to the conference, and out of more than 58,000 names on The Wall, she knew Brian McGar and his family. Amazing!

During the course of the week, Marilyn and I got to know each other better, and she was able to give me information her local paper had printed in stories over the years concerning Brian.

So, 30 years after I met that girl who was wearing an MIA bracelet with Brian McGar's name on it, that part of my life has come full circle. Brian Kent McGar is no longer just a name on The Wall. And, I still have the bracelet.

Brian Kent McGar's status was updated from MIA to KIA on Panel 21E, Line 23 on The Wall.

Arthur Drescher lives in Glenside, Pa., and continues to volunteer at The Wall.

The Box
By
Ron Edgington

It was late May 1996. Bill Harter and I were on duty as Wall volunteers. It was mid-morning, and visitor flow was increasing. I looked up and saw a group of about 12 high school students approaching. Two were carrying a box. They were silent and looked so serious. I looked at Bill, and he said, "This should be interesting."

Little did we know how interesting!

We learned that this was a senior's elective class on the Vietnam War from a high school in New Jersey. They were accompanied by their teacher, a knowledgeable young lady intent on providing first-hand experience in one of life's difficult lessons. Her students had read about visitor reactions at The Wall and the phenomenon of family, friends, war buddies and schoolchildren leaving very personal items—items that held a deep significance—there.

She had asked students to choose an item that held special meaning in their lives, one that could not be replaced, and to put it into the box. This, she reasoned, would illustrate their personal "loss."

The group stopped near Panel 6W and put the box down. Silently, they formed a semi-circle. Their faces showed stress. Some looked ready to cry; all looked nervous. By now, other visitors were stopping to watch. One by one, the students would reach into the box, retrieve their thing and tell the others its meaning in their life: a little league trophy; a varsity letter; a state track medal.

One last student reached in and pulled out a photo of a "grunt" wearing a flak jacket and helmet and leaning against a bunker of sandbags. "This is my dad, and it is the only picture I have of him in Vietnam," she said. She spoke a few more tearful words, then returned the photo to the box.

By now, the crowd was large and blocking the flow of visitors. But that did not seem too important to us. We were as caught up in the emotion as those students were. As the crowd began to disperse, it was evident by the tissues in view that those kids had not only learned a lesson, they had taught one also. Bill and I knew that we had been a part of "Wall Magic."

I have been a volunteer for over a decade. For me, there is "Wall Magic" every day I am there.

When you have looked into the tear-filled eyes of a family member on his or her first visit…

When you are hugged by a Gold Star Mother…

When you are asked to do a rubbing and are told to "save room on the paper for my other son's name"…

When a 10-year-old tugs on your shirt and looks directly at you and says, "Thank you for fighting"…

When you watch 50 or so middle school students from Hawaii place fresh-cut exotic flowers at EACH panel…

When the widow of a Medal of Honor recipient asks you to help her find her husband's name…

When you have stood alone at the apex at midnight and cried…

…Then you will have a better idea of just what Wall Magic is.

Ron Edgington is a Vietnam veteran and a volunteer at the Vietnam Veterans Memorial. He lives in Lincoln University, Pa.

A Special Visitor:
The Commander in Chief
Pays Tribute

During the nearly week-long series of activities that led up to the 10th anniversary of the Memorial in November 1992, one of the most important events was the Reading of the Names. This had never before been done at The Wall.

After a few dignitaries and VIPs started off the reading to the waiting press, the cameras were turned off and the really important people began the nearly 72-hour process. These were the people with strong, personal connections to The Wall. The audience for this emotional event varied by the time of day, from several hundred in the pleasant daylight hours to several dozen in the cold, damp, early November pre-dawn hours.

It was after 11 p.m. one evening. The crowds were small, and the scene was peaceful, until a group of well-dressed individuals caused a disruption. A young lady who had signed up to read names was being asked by these strangers if she would share her names with "the president." This lady was not from the Washington, D.C. area and responded by asking what he was the president of. The presidential handler made it clear that he was referring to the 41st president of the United States, George H.W. Bush. Still, she resisted, because the names she was reading were special to her.

Hearing her response, the president edged past his assistant and talked with her directly. Basically, he said: "I don't want to read your special names, but are there any on your list who you don't know personally that you might share with me?"

The answer was yes. So, when the time came, this volunteer, along with President George H.W. Bush and First

Lady Barbara Bush, proceeded onto the stage to read the list of names together. At this time of night, the seats were normally fairly empty, but when the president stepped up to read, every seat seemed to be magically filled. The darkness was suddenly bright with camera flashes and television lighting.

But the president was not there for publicity. He raised his hand in a halting motion and asked the assembled press to turn off their lights and cameras. "I'm not here to read for the press," he said. "I'm here to read for these heroes on The Wall." They complied, and he read the brief list of names. Then he thanked the volunteer who shared her names with him and left the stage, staying nearby for a little while afterward to talk with the volunteers and veterans who, like him, had braved the elements to pay tribute to fallen heroes.

Ten years later, another VIP guest visited The Wall during the quiet hours. It was the morning of Veterans Day 2002, the 20th anniversary of The Wall.

Preparations start early for these ceremonies. At 6:30 a.m., Memorial Fund Program Director Holly Rotondi was dismayed to find that the crews setting up the chairs and sound system for the afternoon ceremony were being denied access to the area in front of The Wall. And then she saw why.

"Around 7:30 on a cold, rainy morning, when no one was there to see him, President George W. Bush came to The Wall to pay his respects," she remembered. He lingered for a few moments, left his presidential coin, then talked with some volunteers before going on his way. No members of the press were present.

In the case of the father and the son, both presidents, those who witnessed these private visits were left with a warm feeling. What a great country this is where the highest leader in the land can occasionally join with everyday citizens for a common purpose: to remember those who gave their lives in the service of this country.

The Future:
The Vietnam Veterans Memorial Center

The Future: The Vietnam Veterans Memorial Center

In late 2003, the United States Congress passed legislation, which President George W. Bush signed into law, authorizing the Vietnam Veterans Memorial Center to be built at or near the Memorial. A site was chosen on the National Mall, near the Lincoln Memorial and the Vietnam Veterans Memorial, where this underground education center will be located.

The purpose of this facility is to provide a profound educational experience for interested visitors at the Vietnam Veterans Memorial. The Center will allow visitors to learn the importance of the Memorial, its role in helping to remember those who served and in helping to heal the deep societal divisions resulting from the Vietnam War. The Center will also take a larger view, focusing on the shared values of loyalty, duty, respect, service, honor, integrity and courage that prevail among service members who have served in all of America's conflicts. In this way, the Center will foster an appreciation of those who have served and those who now serve in America's armed forces.

The Memorial Center is currently in the design phase. Architects and exhibit designers are working with the Memorial Fund and the National Park Service (NPS), partners in this project, to fine-tune plans for the building and the exhibits inside. Displays planned for this unique education center include:

- *The Wall of Faces*, a display of photographs of those individuals whose names are on The Wall. Photographs will be shown on the person's birthday.

- *The Collections Wall,* a display of a sampling of the over 100,000 poems, photographs, letters and other memorabilia left at The Wall by visitors—a rich and unique legacy for current and future generations to ponder.

- **Timeline** of military events and key actions that took place during the Vietnam War.

- **History of The Wall**, showing the events that took place in order for the Vietnam Veterans Memorial to be built.

- **Resource Center**, where visitors will have the opportunity to get more in-depth information and study various aspects of the war and the era.

As visitors leave the Center, they will see one final display: the **Legacy of Service**. This display will showcase images of individuals who served in all of America's wars—from the Revolutionary War to Iraq and Afghanistan. This display will continue the important legacy of teaching young people about the sacrifices of those who served when called on by their country, and it will provide historical context as visitors leave the Center to experience the rest of the National Mall.

While the Center will not be a museum, it will have creative and stimulating exhibits for the public. Similar visitor centers are at the Lincoln and Jefferson Memorials.

The new structure is being designed to strike a harmonious balance with the three-acre Memorial site. The Memorial Center is estimated to cost between $75 million and $100 million to build, and all of the funds will come from private donations. The Campaign to Build the Vietnam Veterans Memorial Center is being led by Chairman Dr. Christos M. Cotsakos and Honorary Chairman Gen. Colin Powell, USA (Ret.). The Memorial Fund expects to have the money raised and break ground by 2010. The Center will be open 18 months after that.

Vietnam Veterans Memorial Fund

Established in 1979, the Vietnam Veterans Memorial Fund is the nonprofit organization authorized by Congress to build the Vietnam Veterans Memorial in Washington, D.C. Today, it works to preserve the legacy of The Wall, to promote healing and to educate about the impact of the Vietnam War through the following programs:

Ceremonies at The Wall are held each year on Memorial Day and Veterans Day to remember and honor those Americans who served in the armed forces. The Memorial Fund also holds ceremonies to honor veterans and their families on Mother's Day, Father's Day and during the winter holidays.

In Memory honors those who died as a result of the Vietnam War, but whose deaths do not fit the parameters for inclusion on The Wall. A special ceremony is held on the third Monday of April each year.

The Wall That Heals brings the healing power of The Wall to cities and hometowns across America. The traveling half-scale replica of The Wall is accompanied by a traveling museum about the Vietnam War, The Wall and the era.

Echoes From The Wall is a curriculum kit sent free of charge to every middle and high school in America. It provides students not only with historical information about the Vietnam War, but also with an understanding of leadership, citizenship, patriotism and character.

Echoes From The Mall is a field trip guide that helps teachers interpret the Vietnam Veterans Memorial for their students. A wide variety of suggested on-site and classroom activities offer educators a framework for exploring all elements of the Memorial.

The Legacy of The Wall is a traveling storyboard that addresses several different aspects of the Vietnam War and the Memorial, including United States involvement in Vietnam, events on the home front, the history of The Wall and how America honors veterans.

The **Teach Vietnam Teachers Network** is comprised of educators throughout the United States who serve as liaisons between the Memorial Fund, their community and state and local school systems. The Memorial Fund provides members with free educational materials and professional development opportunities.

Volunteers provide assistance to the Memorial's nearly 4 million annual visitors—helping locate names on The Wall, providing history lessons and aiding with name rubbings. The Memorial Fund furnishes the volunteers with the necessary supplies to continue their useful work.

Name Rubbings are provided free. Each week, Memorial Fund volunteers bring paper and pencil to The Wall and begin the work to keep alive the memories of American heroes who made the ultimate sacrifice decades ago.

Memorial Preservation is a cooperative effort between the Memorial Fund and the National Park Service. The Memorial Fund pays for catastrophic insurance for the Memorial as well as for annual name additions and status changes. It also has hired engineering firms to conduct extensive studies on The Wall. The Memorial Fund keeps granite panels in storage in case of damage to The Wall.

The Vietnam Veterans Memorial Fund is a 501(c)(3) non-profit organization, and its funding comes from grants and gifts from the general public.

If you would like more information on our programs or are interested in supporting the Memorial Fund, please contact us at:

VIETNAM VETERANS MEMORIAL FUND
1023 15th Street, NW, Second Floor
Washington, DC 20005
(202) 393-0090 *phone*
(202) 393-0029 *fax*
vvmf@vvmf.org
www.vvmf.org